Love Your Canary

Roy Stringer

W. Foulsham & Co. Ltd.

London ● New York ● Toronto ● Cape Town ● Sydney

F

2118303J

Page 2: Fife (Variegated)

W. Foulsham & Company Limited
Yeovil Road, Slough, Berkshire, SL1 4JH

ISBN 0–572–01367–1

Printed in Spain by Cayfosa. Barcelona
Dep. Leg. B-11517-1986

Contents

1 The Decision to Keep a Canary

So you think you would like to keep a canary? Have you thought what this involves? Keeping a pet of any kind is a responsibility. A canary must be fed and watered every day and cleaned out at least once a week. If you go away on holiday someone must be found to do these jobs for you. A canary needs a good cage and this will cost money; so will the equipment such as drinkers and feeders.

Yet keeping a canary will give you a lot of pleasure. Canaries are lively birds which are forever active; moving about from perch to perch. The song of the cock canary is beautiful. If you decide to keep several canaries you will be able to breed from them and it can turn into an interesting hobby if you go to bird shows and meet other canary breeders.

2 **Housing a Canary**

Whether you are going to buy a pet canary, or more than one for breeding, it is best to have a cage ready for when you arrive home. This will mean that the bird will be put straight into its own home and not be disturbed by being kept in some temporary housing.

If you are going to keep a pet canary in the house there are lots of designs of cage available in pet shops. Nearly all of them will house your canary safely and comfortably. It is best to buy the largest cage you can afford, remembering that it has to fit in one of your rooms at home. Cages with plastic bottoms, which can be removed, are easily disinfected. Cages with metal bottoms can become rusty after a time. The standard round perches, fitted in most pet cages, are not the best for canaries. Twigs with diameters varying between 9.5mm and 12mm (3/8 inch and 1/2 inch) are better. The different diameters exercise the bird's feet. But perches are easily changed, so if you find a cage which suits you, do not be put off by the perches. Change them.

If you want to breed canaries you will need a double breeding cage. This can be made quite easily from plywood and two wire cage fronts bought from a pet shop. For canaries it is best to buy wire fronts which have small doors which slide up and down. Although some breeders use slightly smaller cages, an ideal size is 76cm long, 40cm high and 25cm from front to back. (30 inches × 16 inches × 10 inches) Cages deeper than 25cm (10 inches) deep encourage canaries to move to the back of the cage when you are looking at them. This can be a problem if ever you want to show your birds.

When making a double breeding cage, leave a small gap between the two wire fronts. A gap the same as the distance between the

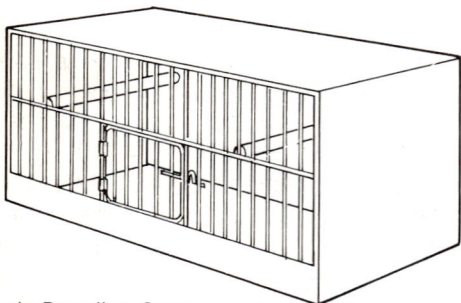

Single Breeding Cage

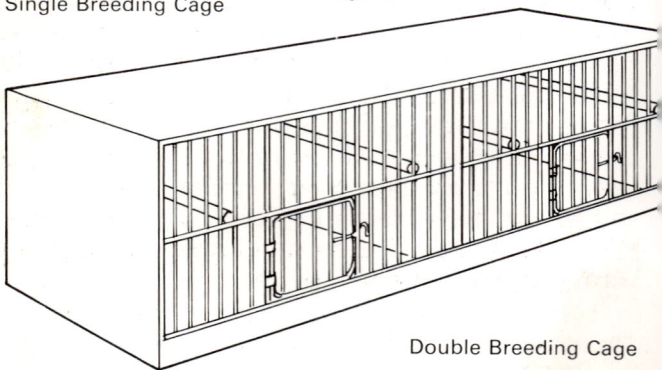

Double Breeding Cage

wires of the cage front is about right. A piece of wire netting can be slid in to divide the cage into two compartments when it is needed. Twigs can be used as perches in breeding cages, but if you keep the round ones you can make grooves in them by dragging a hacksaw blade along the length of the perch. This will make it easier for a canary to grip firmly. Oval perches can be bought and these are very good.

When choosing which colour to paint the inside of your canary breeding cage it is as well to choose one which will show off your birds at their best. Pale green and pale blue are very popular.

If you have a garden an aviary is an ideal place to house and breed canaries. The size of the aviary will depend on the size of your garden and how many birds you intend to keep. A wooden frame 1.8m × 1.8m × 1.2m (6 feet × 6 feet × 4 feet) covered with 12mm (½ inch) wire netting will comfortably house a breeding colony of three cocks and six hens. Welded wire mesh 25mm × 12mm (1 inch × ½ inch) is a good alternative to netting. 19 gauge (thickness) wire is thick enough, but 16 gauge is better. Wire fixed on to both the inside and the outside of the frame acts as a protection against cats or, in some areas, hawks. If you can afford only one covering of netting a more attractive appearance is made by fixing the wire to the inside of the frame. Your canaries will also need a waterproof and draughtproof shelter to sleep in.

This can form one end of the flight and for the size of aviary described a depth of 0.6m (2 feet) would be large enough. The shelter

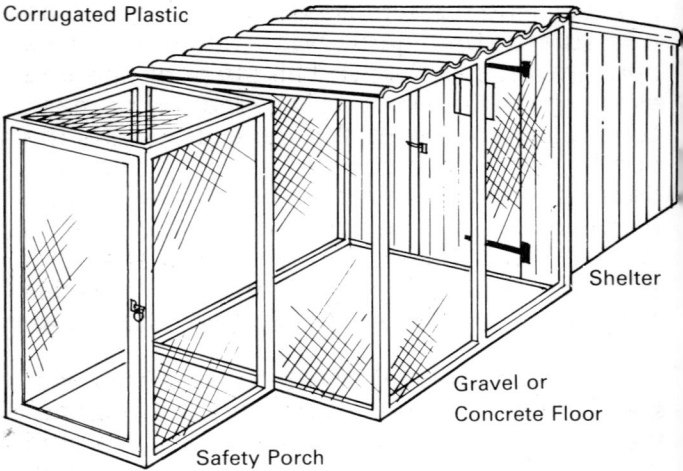

Corrugated Plastic

Shelter

Gravel or Concrete Floor

Safety Porch

Outside Aviary

should have a large door into the flight, which can be opened in warm weather and for cleaning out, and a small door 15cm- 6 inches square will do for the birds to get from the shelter to the flight when the large door is closed. Both doors can be closed when the canaries have gone inside to roost for the night. The shelter must be fitted with plenty of perches so that every bird can find a place it likes. In the flight, small branches from fruit trees can be used as perching. Do not use the wood from other trees.

You will need to take care when building the door from the garden into the flight, which you will need to use when you go in to feed, clean out or even just stand admiring your canaries. You must make sure that the birds do not fly past you and escape as you are going in. The first rule is that flight doors should always open inwards so that you fill the door opening as you go in. Safest of all is a small, wire-mesh covered porch. With this, you step into the porch, close the first door and then open the door into the flight. If you do not have a porch, then a door only about 1m high (3 feet 3 inches) can be used. You will find that as you enter the canaries will fly up and away and this will give you time to get in without any escaping.

The roof of the flight should be covered with sheets of corrugated plastic. This will keep out the droppings of wild birds – which could carry disease – and be a further protection against cats and hawks. Garden soil and lawn are not suitable floors for canary flights. They soon become messy and are very difficult to clean. Best are either concrete or a thick layer of gravel which can be washed with a hose pipe.

3 Equipment

The equipment you need for your cage consists mainly of feeding utensils. Canaries do not need the toys which are made for other types of birds. You can use dishes and bowls not made specially for canaries, but it is better to use drinkers and feeders which have been specially designed.

If you give water in an open dish, inside the cage, it will soon become full of seed husks and droppings. It will not then be clean enough for your canary to drink. Your pet will also bathe in the water when you do not want it to get wet. You also have to open the cage door to put the water dish in the cage. The best utensil for giving water is either a plastic water fountain or a small external, open drinker, both of which clip on to the outside of the cage. The part of the water fountain inside the cage is too small for your canary to be able to bathe when you do not want it to. If you want to use an outside, open drinker there needs to be a small opening in the cage wires; large enough for the canary to put its head through to drink, but not so large that it can escape. The open dish, supplied with the cage, can be used for grit. The same sort of drinkers can be used on breeding cages, but if you keep several pairs in a flight you need something which will hold more

Open Dishes

Bottle Drinker

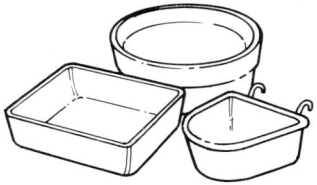

Feeder For Seed and Water

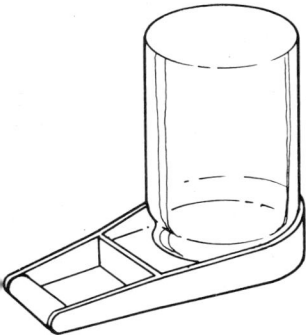

Jar-type Feeder

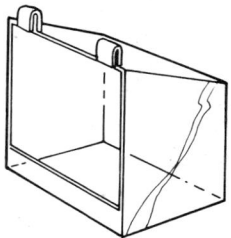

Bath

water. You can buy a galvanised base which holds a plastic lemonade bottle. This is a standard animal drinker.

An open dish is better for seed than for water, but still has the problems that droppings can get in with the seed and the cage door has to be opened for refilling. A larger version of the water fountain can be bought, with the same advantages. When using with seed, you should read the instructions carefully. There is a gap in the plastic tube which needs to be lined up with the feeding outlet so that the seed can flow freely. In breeding cages and flights you may need something larger. There are many types of seed hopper on the market. One which works well with canaries has a plastic base on which you can stand a glass jar. It is best to buy a clip to hold a piece of cuttle fish bone which is good for canaries. This stops the bone getting dirty by lying around on the cage floor.

Canaries love to have a bath. Specially designed baths can be bought from pet shops which fit over the cage door opening. The advantage of these is that you can decide the best time for your pet to bathe – and the rest of the cage does not get wet.

4 Selecting the Variety

Canaries were first brought to Europe, from the Canary Islands, over 400 years ago. At first, the attraction of the small birds was their song rather than their appearance. They were about 10cm (4 inches) in length and were dark green in colour.

Today there is a wide variety of sizes and colours available – and the canary's song is still as beautiful. In fact, German canary breeders bred a type of canary, called the Roller, which sings even better than the wild birds. In other parts of Europe, breeders bred canaries for their shape and colour. Some are named after the area of Britain where they were bred, such as the Gloster, Norwich, Fife and Border. Border canaries were first bred on the borders of Scotland and England.

When selecting which canary to keep as a pet, there are far more important things to consider than the variety. Any cock canary will sing and Chapter 5 explains how to choose a healthy bird. If your interest is in breeding canaries then it is worth considering that some varieties are easier to manage than others. Rollers, Fifes, Borders, Glosters and Coloured canaries are good varieties to start with. Larger canaries, such as Norwich and Yorkshire, are best left until you have gained some experience. Even with the "easier" varieties, some care has to be taken when choosing which cock to pair with which hen. Chapter 10 explains what to do.

The following information will help you to identify some of the different varieties of canary.

The Border

The Border canary is the oldest of the varieties bred for its shape. Its ideal length is 14.6cm (5¾ inches) and its most desirable feature is its roundness. A good Border has a round head on a round body. Borders are lively birds; always on the move.

The Fife

The Fife canary has been developed by breeders who felt that Border canaries were getting too large. The Fife is best described as a miniature Border and should be no longer than 11.4cm (4½ inches).

The Gloster

There are two types of Gloster canary; Coronas and Consorts. The Gloster Corona is the most distinctive because it has a crest on top of its head. Consorts do not have a crest. Although Glosters are among the smaller canaries at 11.4cm (4½ inches) long, the better ones are thickset and well-built.

The Norwich

The Norwich canary is a large bird, well-built and stocky. A wide, round head – with feath-

Clear Border

ering forming a cap over the eyes – is attached to a short body by a thick neck. It is not a good variety to begin with.

The Yorkshire

The Yorkshire is another large canary. It is longer than the Norwich and stands more upright. For this reason it is sometimes called "The Guardsman". It is another variety which is best left to the experts.

The Lizard

The Lizard canary was developed for its markings. Its body and wings have a dark pattern and the name was chosen because there is some resemblance to a lizard's scales. The beauty of the Lizard is the contrast between these dark feathers and the clear cap on top of the head. If the cap has some dark feathers it is known as a broken-cap. A Lizard with no clear feathers on its head is called a non-cap. According to its colour a Lizard canary is called a Gold or a Silver.

The Roller

Roller canaries are the variety which was developed for its song alone. The best came from southern Germany. Their shape is not important, nor is their colour. Rollers tend to be slim.

Coloured Canaries

Although paying some attention to shape and size, Coloured canary breeders pay most attention to the colour of their birds. A very wide

Cinnamon Border
Green Border

only one. You do not want the chicks to become wild, flying from one perch to another. They can damage their claws when they contact a perch at speed. By the time the chicks are self-supporting, the cock and hen will be part way through the same cycle as the first round. Your management should be the same as in the first round.

If the birds are fit, they will sometimes go on breeding for three rounds. You must not permit them to attempt to produce a fourth. The nest should be removed and the cock and hen separated.

12 Showing Canaries

If you are interested in canaries, other than as pets, a bird show is the place to go. Some shows are advertised in local newspapers, but to find out what clubs and shows are in your area you should buy *Cage and Aviary Birds*. This is a weekly paper which deals with all aspects of birdkeeping and carries up-to-date news of club meetings and shows.

Once you have located your local cage bird society or specialist canary society you may choose to join. Cage bird societies cater for all varieties of canaries, but there are specialist clubs which deal with only one variety; Borders, Glosters, Norwich, Coloured etc. By comparing your canaries with other members' you will get some idea whether your birds are the type which can win prizes. The larger the show you go to, the wider the varieties of canaries you will see – and generally, the larger the show fhe better the quality of the birds. You will notice that the canaries on show are in good feather condition. Breeders go to a lot of trouble to make sure that their canaries are in perfect feather for a show. No judge will give a prize to a bird whose feathers are dirty and uneven.

Each variety of canary has a governing body

which lays down a standard of excellence for the variety. In some varieties it is the shape of the canary which is most important. These are called "type" canaries and include Borders, Glosters and Norwich. Others, such as the Coloured Canary, are judged much more on their colour.

With different bodies laying down the rules it is not possible to list a general set of rules applying to canaries as a whole. In any case, rules are changed year by year — even to the desirable shape and size of the ideal canary. Each body has its own rules for appointing judges. Some have to take an examination on judging while others merely have to have kept canaries, exhibit them and be a Champion.

Shows are divided into sections for Champions and Novices so that newcomers do not have to show their birds against breeders who have kept canaries for many years. Although the time varies, a Novice should become a Champion about five years after beginning to show his canaries.

Canaries are shown in classes according to their colour and age. Young birds are shown in "unflighted" classes and old birds in "flighted" classes. In the Gloster Canary section, Coronas are in different classes to Consorts. The winner of each class is judged against all of the others to find the best Canary in its section. Sometimes the best of each canary section compete to decide which is the best canary in show.

The canary show season runs from September through into January. If you decide to enter a show, you must obtain a standard show cage for the variety to be shown. All of the cages for a particular variety of canary are

Coloured – Non-intensive Red (frosted)

the same so that no exhibitor gains an advantage. Club shows, staged just for club members, are usually easy going affairs, where you can turn up with your birds and enter them on the day. The Show Secretary will help you to put them in the correct classes. Open shows are more formal and your birds need to be entered in advance. When you find a show you would like to show at, send for a schedule. Ask an experienced breeder for help on which classes your birds should be entered in. Otherwise you might arrive at the show, after judging, to see "W/C" written on your cage. This means "wrong class" and that the bird has not been judged. A few days before the show your cage labels will arrive through the post. Make sure that you stick the correct label to the correct cage before taking your canaries to the show hall. The schedule will show what time your birds need to be delivered to be in time for judging. It will also show what time the show opens to the public, so that you can return to see if your birds have won a prize. Better still, ask if you can help at the show, when you send in your entry form. If you do, you must be prepared for hard work, but the whole day will be spent with, and talking about canaries. What better way is there to spend a day?

I hope that after reading this book you decide that you would still like to keep a canary – or even several canaries – and that the information you have read will help you to keep fit, happy and healthy pets.

Consort Gloster — Variegated

Useful Addresses

Cage and Aviary Birds
Surrey House
1 Throwley Way
Sutton
Surrey SM1 4QQ

The Secretary
The Border Canary Convention
29 Penfold Lane
Great Billing
Northants.

Yorkshire Buff — Variegated

range of shades has been developed on what is the newest variety. The most striking shades, such as Red and Bronze, are improved by feeding special foods. Coloured canaries are easy to manage but correct colour feeding and being able to recognise the different types needs experience.

With the exception of Coloured canaries, the colours seen on canaries are not as vivid as those seen on more exotic birds. What they lack in vividness they make up for in the gentleness of the shades. A green canary – of whatever variety – is a deep grass green over-laid with black markings, like pencil lines. Its beak, legs and claws are black. A blue canary has the same dark markings, but this time on a slate blue background.

When breeders talk about their canaries they use words which are not always easy to understand. The following list will help you:

Clear: Without any dark feathers.

Self: One dark colour all over.

Variegated: Having some dark feathers.

Cinnamon: Having brown instead of black markings.

Yellow: This can refer to the colour of a canary, but more often describes the feather texture of a bird. Yellow feathers are small and the colour of the feather goes from quill to tip. Yellow feathered birds are usually bright in colour.

Consort Gloster

Buff: This describes the feather type opposite to Yellow. Buff feathers are broad and coarse. Their colour does not reach the tip and so a white frosting can be seen. Buff feathered birds tend to be pale in colour.

Flighted: A flighted canary is more than one year old.

Unflighted: An unflighted canary is less than one year old.

5 Buying a Canary

Before going out to buy a canary, you should make up your mind where your interest lies. Do you want a pet, which will brighten up your home with its lovely song, or do you want to breed canaries?

If it is a pet you want, you must buy a cock bird; preferably a young one. A hen will make a pet, but will not reward your attention with its song. When canaries are young it is not always easy to tell which are cocks and which are hens. An experienced pet shop owner or breeder of canaries will be able to help you. Sexing older canaries is easier. Cocks tend to be bolder, brighter birds and they sing from the stomach. Hens give a double "chirp" and sometimes a short trill from the throat. If you particularly want a certain variety, it can be best to go to a breeder who specialises in the variety.

The cost of a canary will vary with the variety. In general, Borders, Glosters and Rollers will be at the cheaper end of the scale. You will find Norwich and Yorkshires are more expensive. No matter what type of canary you decide to buy, they will still vary with the quality of the bird in question and who is selling it.

What to look for when buying a pet canary

When you think you have found the canary you would like as a pet, take a good look at it and check out several things:

1. Is the bird a cock?
   If you cannot tell from the song, ask the help of an experienced breeder.
2. Is the bird young?
   The age of your pet canary is not important, except that the younger it is when you buy it, the more years you will have to love it. A canary with scales on its legs is almost certain to be older than one year. Very long claws can also show that a bird is not young.
3. Is it healthy?
   A canary which looks happy and bright, moving about busily, is a fit bird. A wide-open bright eye is another good sign. Any bird which sits quietly, with its eyes partly closed and feathers fluffed up, should not be bought.
4. Are the feathers under the vent clean?
   If a bird has dirty vent feathers it may have a stomach upset. It is best left and another one chosen.

What to look for when buying canaries to breed

If you are buying canaries to breed from, it is best to choose cocks and hens which are about twelve months old and have never been used for breeding. Birds more than two years old may not be such successful breeders and you will have less opportunity to breed from them before they become too old.

Corona Gloster
Corona Gloster – Grizzle

When buying canaries, you should ask how old each bird is. Signs of old age are scaly legs on both cocks and hens. Checks 2–4 for choosing which pet canary to buy also apply to breeding birds. You should also check:

a) Is the bird the variety you want?

By using the descriptions and photographs in this book you will be able to recognise most varieties of canary. If you are not sure you should ask the help of an experienced breeder. You should not pair a cock of one variety with a hen of another. There is no purpose in mixing the varieties, when breeders have spent many years making each have its own characteristics.

b) Is the bird the sex you want?

As explained before, it is the song which shows whether a canary is a cock or a hen. Never be afraid to ask for the advice of someone who breeds canaries.

c) Are the birds legs and claws well-formed?

A typical problem with canaries' claws is a sprain, called "stiff hind claw". This causes one of the rear claws to stick out straight. Although this would not matter if the bird was a pet, for breeding you should not use canaries with faults.

6 **Food and Water**

Seed

The basic food a canary needs is a mixture of plain canary seed and either black or red rape seed. You should mix two parts of canary seed with one part of the rape seed. The two seeds together contain the foods which will keep your pet fit. But no-one likes to eat the same meal all of the time and so later in this chapter you will read of other foods which your canary will enjoy.

When you go to buy a supply of seed, you will see a brown seed which is pointed at both ends. This is plain canary seed. Rape seed is round in shape. Black rape seed is in its natural state. Red rape seed has been boiled. Canaries enjoy both.

Every few weeks you can add a small amount of linseed to the mixture. This is an oily seed and helps to put a shine on a bird's feathering. If a bird eats too much oily seed it can become fat. Most pet shops sell a seed mixture for canaries, containing more seeds than those mentioned above. You can offer some of this to your canary. What often happens is that a bird will eat only some of the seeds and leaves the rest. This is wasteful and can also make you think that your pet has plenty of seed in its feeder when, in fact, it needs to be refilled.

It is usually cheaper to buy loose seed at a pet shop. If you have several canaries you can buy seed in larger amounts. The more seed you buy at one time, the less it will cost to feed your birds. A canary needs to have seed available at all times.

Water

A canary needs to be able to have a drink of water whenever it wants it. If water is not available for even a short time a canary can suffer and become unwell. From time to time you can add a vitamin additive or tonic to the drinking water. These can be bought from good pet shops. When adding anything to your canary's water always read the instructions carefully and do not add more than the stated amount. Canaries are small birds and require only small amounts of additives. You will find that canaries drink more water than most other birds.

Grit

Canaries need a supply of grit so that they can digest their food. When they eat seeds, they remove the husk and swallow the kernel whole. A store of grit, kept in the crop, grinds up the seeds before they pass further into the digestive system. Grit comes in the form of Mineral Grit and Oystershell Grit. Both work equally well.

It is thought that grit which is too sharp can damage the inside of a canary's crop and so it is best to buy a good brand which has been specially prepared for canaries.

Cuttlefish Bone

Canaries like to peck at a piece of cuttlefish bone. They benefit from the calcium they consume as this helps to make their bones strong. Breeding hens need calcium to form the shells of the eggs they lay.

Iodine Block

Canaries are not so keen as some other birds to peck at an iodine block. But the blocks do not cost very much and so it is worth buying one for your pet. By pecking at an iodine block a canary will consume iodine and minerals which will help to keep it healthy.

Greenfood

Canaries love to eat greenfood, but you must be very careful when feeding it. The cheapest form of greenfood is dandelion leaves and chickweed, but there is a risk involved when using these. If wild greens have been sprayed, to kill weeds or insects, they can be dangerous to feed to your canary. There is also a risk that a cat or dog has used the ground around the weeds as a toilet.

Any greens should be washed and dried before feeding to your birds. So it is best to feed greens which you grow yourself or buy at a greengrocers. Lettuce, spinach and cress are suitable. Greens should be fed early in the day and in small quantities. They are absorbed quickly into the digestive system and if fed in the evening can lead to a bird spending the night with an empty crop. The remains of greens should be removed from the cage the same day that they are given to avoid the eating of stale food.

Treats

As well as their basic diet canaries love to sample other sorts of food as a treat. Small slices of carrot or fresh fruit, such as sweet apple or orange, are good for canaries. Any left over should be removed the same day.

Although some canaries will eat many types of food, there are some which are best avoided, except in very small quantities. Bread, cake and biscuits can quickly make a canary fat. A fat bird is not a fit bird.

One treat, which can be useful when your canary is a little off-colour or when a hen is feeding chicks, is bread and milk. Dampen a small piece of stale, wholemeal bread with boiled milk. A sprinkling of maw seed will encourage your bird to eat it.

To sum up; a canary must have seed, water and grit – especially water – available all of the time. Care should be taken that greenfood is clean and dry. Some extra foods can make a canary fat.

7 General Management

The management of a canary — or several canaries — is very simple. It need take only a few minutes each day, with an extra effort once a week when cleaning out. This means that, when you buy a canary, you will be able to look after it properly and still have plenty of time to enjoy its company.

You need to find a good position for your canary's cage. A cool, airy place is best, so avoid draughts and direct sunshine. This means that placing a cage in a window is *not* a good idea. Being placed in a draught can cause a canary to become ill. It is better to place the cage in a room where the temperature stays steady. Central heating radiators, coming on and going off, can cause a canary to go into a soft moult. This will stop him singing.

The position of seed and water feeders is also important. Seed and water must never be placed in a position where your birds droppings can get into them. Under a perch is the *worst* possible place. The same is true of any other item you put into the cage, such as cuttlefish bone, greens and fruit. Find a position where they will stay clean.

Both seed and water need your attention

every day. The water container should be washed and then rinsed thoroughly before being refilled with fresh water. When a fountain type feeder is used for seed, it should be checked every day to see that there is plenty of seed inside and that the outlet for the seed is not blocked. Seed husks are not usually a problem with this type of feeder. If it looks as though the level of seed has not gone down, check at once. This can mean that there is a blockage and that your canary cannot get at its seed. When seed is fed in an open dish the empty seed husks tend to lie on top. These need to be blown off every day, taking care not to get a seed husk in your eye. When the seed husks are gone you will be able to see how much seed is left in the dish. Even then, check once more as sometimes you will find a layer of dust in the bottom of the dish. Fill up the seed dish every day. A pet canary will sleep better if you place a piece of light cloth over its cage late in the evening.

Not all canary owners let their pets out of their cages so that they can fly around the room. If you decide to do so there are several things to check to make sure that it will be safe. Make sure that all doors and windows are closed. If you have an open fireplace, make sure that it is guarded. Pull the curtain across any clear glass windows, or your pet, not knowing that there is any glass there, will fly into it and may damage itself. If you have a cat or a dog make sure that they are not in the room.

A food treat may tempt your pet back into its cage, when it decides that it has enjoyed enough freedom. If not you have more of a

Norwich – Clear
Norwich – Variegated

32

problem. First darken the room, which will permit you to get close without your pet flying off. Then throw a soft cloth over it to capture it. When handling a canary, you must always be very gentle and not use too much pressure. When being held, its wings should be in their natural position, folded to the body. Remember always to be very gentle.

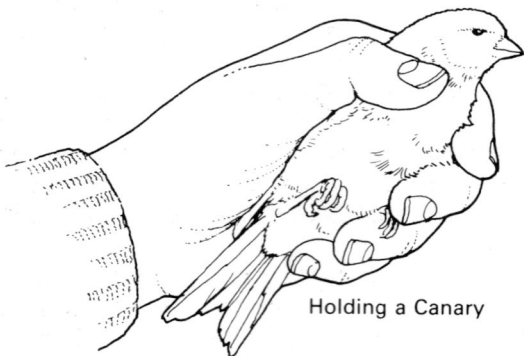

Holding a Canary

8 **Cleaning Out**

Any pet needs to be cleaned out regularly. It depends on you to keep its housing and equipment clean. Canaries need to be cleaned out at least once a week. You can buy sandpaper sheets from a pet shop which make cleaning out very simple, as far as the floor of the cage is concerned. It is just a matter of removing the old sheet and putting a new sheet in its place. If your canary pecks at the sheet, it will do it no harm.

It is a little cheaper to use bird sand on the floor of a cage, but it takes a little more time to remove the sand and replace it. In breeding cages, wood shavings are often used to cover the cage floor. These are not so good in pet cages as they tend to come out of the cage when the canary flutters its wings. If you do decide to use wood shavings, buy them from a pet shop. Shavings bought from a wood yard may have been treated with chemicals which could make your bird ill. The cheapest of all cage floor coverings is a piece of newspaper. This works well but does not look as attractive as the others.

About once a month you should disinfect the cage and equipment. Use a mild disinfectant and rinse feeders and water containers well in clean water before refilling them. Disinfectant should be used more often if a canary has a stomach upset and its droppings are green instead of the normal black and white.

Perches need special attention when cleaning out. They can become very dirty with the bird's own droppings which, if left, get hard and could damage a canary's feet. Perches should be scrubbed with disinfectant, rinsed and dried before being put back in the cage.

9 **Illness and Disease**

Canaries are quite hardy and can stand a fairly wide range of conditions without becoming ill. Some item of food – causing a stomach upset – or being placed in a draught, bringing on a cold – are the most usual forms of illness. They are naturally bright, active birds and so the first sign of illness can be that they sleep longer than usual. A small change to the diet or position of the cage at this stage can stop 'the illness going any further. But if your canary reaches the stage where it is huddled up on the floor of the cage, it is time to get the advice of a vet.

Enteritis

Stomach upsets are the most common form of illness in canaries. The appearance of a bird and its droppings are both signs that a canary is suffering from enteritis. A slight case will see a canary sitting quietly, feathers fluffed up rather than smooth. It will sleep more than usual, with its head under its wing. The droppings will be green rather than the normal black and white and will be wetter than usual. In a severe case, the fluffing up will be to a point where the bird's head seems to be withdrawn into its body and its eyes will be closed. The bird's droppings will be coating its tail and its vent. The change in the droppings is the most certain sign that something is wrong, because it is easy to mistake a canary going to sleep, with its head under its wing, for illness. You will soon get used to seeing what a healthy canary looks like and it is the changes from this that you should be looking for.

The first steps in treating any case of stomach upset is to move the bird to a warm place and remove any food other than the seed mixture. Green food is often the cause of enteritis, particularly if it is stale, dirty, wet or has been subject to frost. So make sure that your bird eats no green food while it is ill. Even when your bird is well all green food should be taken from the cage at the end of each day so that it cannot be eaten when it is stale. Bread and milk may help your canary to get better. Pour boiling milk on to a small piece of bread and leave it to get cool before offering it to your pet. If it does not eat it, a little maw seed sprinkled on top will make it more attractive. Pet shops sell medicines which can be put in a canary's drinking water. In slight cases of stomach upsets, one of these can be tried for a couple of days. If the bird gets no better then you should consult a vet. In serious cases it is best to speak to a vet straight away.

Sickness

Sometimes, a canary will bring back some food which does not suit it. This does not happen very often and the bird usually returns

Yorkshire — Clear
Yorkshire — Variegated

to normal within a couple of days. If not, consult a vet or experienced canary breeder. A cock canary feeds his mate when he is in breeding condition, so be careful not to mistake this for being sick.

Moult

Moulting cannot be called an illness as it is just a case of a bird dropping its old feathers so that it can grow new ones. In the wild, this happens once a year, but the changes of temperature in a house can cause it to happen more often. A bird which is moulting is more likely to become ill so extra care must be taken. It should be kept in a temperature as constant as possible and a tonic in the drinking water can help. Small extras of food can give a moulting canary a boost, such as hard-boiled egg, carrot, apple or sweet biscuit.

Feather Plucking

Unlike some other birds, canaries do not often pluck the feathers out of their young. If you have several canaries in the same cage together they will play at pulling each others' feathers out. A bald patch at the back of a canary's head can show that there are mite in its cage, which get on to the bird and irritate it.

Mite

If cages are kept clean and disinfected, mite should not be a problem. If you bring chickweed into a cage, when the weather is very dry, it can bring mite with it. If your canary begins to peck itself and shakes its feathers it

Lizard – Gold Cap

may have mite. Pet shops sell powders and sprays which can be used on both birds and equipment. If a bird has mite, these get rid of them very quickly.

Beaks and Claws

Sometimes a canary's beak and claws can become overgrown. If your bird has a piece of cuttlefish bone to peck, its beak should not be a problem. Some pet shops sell perches with sandpaper fixed to the underside. These can help to keep claws the correct length. The cutting of claws is best left to experts. At the centre of claws are blood vessels and cutting by an inexperienced person can cause bleeding to occur. If you do cut a claw, check where the blood vessel stops – by holding up to the light – and cut no closer than 3mm (⅛ inch) to this.

Egg Binding

Occasionally, when breeding, a canary hen becomes egg bound. If a hen looks bright and alert it is *not* egg bound. An egg bound hen looks fluffed up and unwell; often sitting on the floor of the cage. Keeping a hen warm is often all that is required for it to pass the egg. If not, make a syrup from sugar and water and put a small amount in the bird's beak. Egg binding is usually a problem only with fat hens. Canaries which have plenty of exercise and are fed on a healthy diet do not become egg bound.

Injuries

Injuries, such as broken legs and wings, should be treated as quickly as possible by a vet. If you buy a bird which has a ring on its leg, ask the breeder to remove it. As a canary grows older it grows scales on its legs and a ring which is loose when the bird is young may become tight and cause problems when it is older.

General

Never be afraid to ask advice of an experienced breeder if you are worried that your canary may be ill. When giving medicine in the drinking water always make sure that the dose is that stated on the bottle and take away any other drinking water.

10 **Breeding**

Canaries are like native finches in that they breed at a certain time of the year. As the days get longer and the weather gets warmer the desire to breed is triggered off in both cocks and hens. In Britain, this usually occurs around the end of March, but there are differences between the south and north of the country. If you intend your canaries to breed, it is best to start conditioning them from January onwards. Pet shops sell egg food mixtures, which can be fed to canaries when damped with water. Breeders call this softfood. If you give a small amount of softfood to your birds, starting with once a week in January and increasing to three times a week in March it will give them the strength to breed.

You can also buy 'Condition seed', a mixture which experience has shown brings canaries into breeding condition. Again, a small amount once a week in January, increasing to three times a week in March is the correct amount. It is best to avoid any artificial lighting in a breeding room or aviary as it may bring your canaries into condition at the wrong time. Then you will have a very poor breeding season.

The way in which your canaries behave will tell you whether they are in breeding condition. Both cocks and hens will be very active. Cocks will stretch and distort their bodies.

Coloured – Intensive Red

Their wings will drop down at each side of their bodies and they will sing frantically. Hens will move quickly from perch to perch, occasionally dropping to the floor to pick up small items, such as a piece of sawdust, in their beaks. This is a sign that the hens are ready to build nests. Canaries should not be permitted to breed if they are younger than ten months old.

The best way to breed canaries is in cages, but some people prefer to let their birds breed in an aviary. In this case it is best to have more hens than cocks in the aviary; say two hens to every cock. This will help to avoid any fighting. You will need to provide more nesting places than hens; say eight nests to six hens. Even then, you may find that two hens will decide to lay their eggs in the same nest and share the duties of incubating the eggs and rearing the chicks.

Types of nesting pan will be described when cage breeding is explained, but when breeding in an aviary, it is best to fix a small platform under each nest so that any chick which falls from the nest will not fall to the aviary floor.

When breeding canaries in an aviary, cocks and hens are together before, during and after breeding. In cages, there is more control to ensure that there is a better chance of breeding the chicks you want. Cage breeding lets you choose which cock will be father of your chicks and which hen will be their mother. In this way you can avoid weakness in the chicks by birds mating which are too closely related. You can also influence the colours which will be bred.

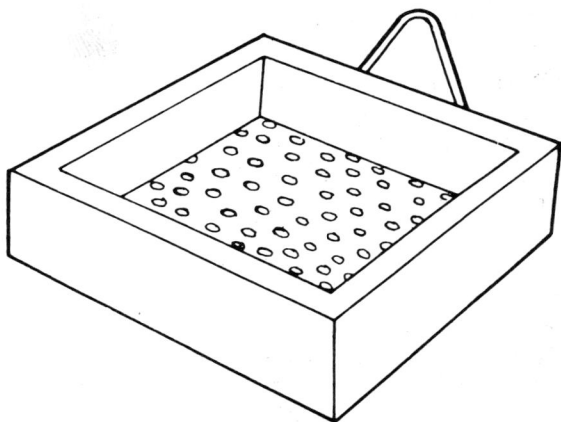

Nesting bowls

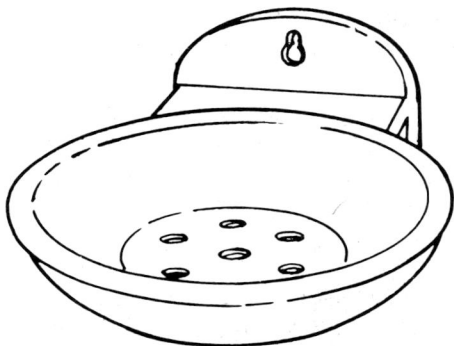

Leading up to the breeding season cocks and hens are kept apart. When both cock and hen, of a chosen pair, are ready to breed they can be put into a double breeding cage with a wire divider separating them. Obviously, each has its own seed and water. When the cock is seen to feed the hen, through the wire, the slide can be removed and a nesting bowl or box can be put into position, high up at one end of the cage, You can buy nesting pans, made from plastic, from a pet shop or you can make them from wood and perforated metal sheet. A frame, 100mm square (4 inches) and about 25mm high (1 inch) with a bottom made of perforated metal works very well. Whichever type you use, you must make certain that it is fixed firmly to the wall of the cage so that it will carry the weight of parent birds and chicks. Nest pan liners made of felt should be fixed inside the pans. These can be glued or stitched in position. It is best to buy these from a pet shop as, if you make them yourself, you may use a material which can injure your birds. The same is true of the nesting material, which you give to your canaries, so that they can build their own nests. Never use any man-made material, such as nylon; the threads are very strong and when wrapped around a canary's leg can be very difficult to remove. The best materials for nest building are dried grasses and moss, wedged in between the cage wires so that the birds can select what they want. To finish the nest cotton wool can be offered. The hens will take it and make a very comfortable lining.

When the hen is ready to be mated, she will crouch on the perch and form her back into a hollow. The cock will step on to the hen's back, place one wing across her neck and tuck his tail under her vent. Eggs are fertilised by the cock bird spraying sperm on to the hen's vent. Firmly fixed perches are essential if mating is to be successful.

11 Eggs and Chicks

If all goes well, your hen will lay her first egg, seven to ten days after you remove the wire slide to let the cock and hen be together. Canary hens lay their eggs every day, usually stopping at four. If the eggs were left with the hen they would hatch at one day intervals and when the fourth chick hatched the oldest would be four days old. It can happen that the younger chicks die, either squashed or neglected in favour of the older chicks which can call louder for food. This is one of the disadvantages of breeding canaries in aviaries and leaving them to themselves. To avoid this problem, most breeders remove each egg as it is laid and replace it with a "dummy" egg. These can be bought from pet shops or you can make your own. Some breeders use small pebbles.

Eggs must always be handled with great care. A teaspoon can be used to lift an egg from the nest. The eggs can be stored in a container, on a bed of sawdust or bran. When several pairs are being used for breeding, separate containers should be used – clearly marked – so that the eggs from one pair do not get mixed up with the eggs from another. Each day, as a new egg is put into the container, those already there must be turned so that the bottom of the egg becomes the top. Eggs are

Coloured – Non-intensive Rose

removed until the evening of the third day. You should now have three eggs which you will put back into the nest; removing the dummy eggs. The next, fourth, morning the hen will lay her fourth egg. Each egg will hatch on the same day and each chick will have an equal chance of survival. If the hen should go on to lay a fifth egg, it will hatch a few hours after the other four, but there will be a fair chance that the chick will survive.

Canaries' eggs are pale blue with brown flecking. At first they are shiny and you can see through the shell when an egg is held up to the light. If the egg is not fertile it will stay in this condition. If it is fertile it will become solid in appearance and take on a matt finish. On the evening of the 13th day after returning the eggs, give the breeding pair half a teaspoonful of softfood. The eggs should hatch on the 14th day. If the cock seems to be paying too much attention to the nest, during the 14 days that the hen is incubating the eggs, it may be best to put him back into the half of the cage he occupied at first and refit the wire divider. He can be returned when the chicks are about ten days old. He will help to feed the chicks. Softfood can be given twice a day. It is better to give small quantities regularly rather than large amounts which can become stale.

When chicks hatch, it is best to have a perch positioned slightly above the nest and 15mm (⅝ inch) away. Sometimes a small chick can get caught up in its mother's feathering and be lifted out of the nest. This perch brushes the chick back into the nest and helps to prevent it falling to the cage floor. For the first few days of canaries' lives they pass their droppings in

Coloured – Bronze

52

small, sealed sacs. The hen eats these up and passes them with her own droppings. This is a habit developed in the wild, where it prevents any small animals, searching for food, knowing that they are there. At about ten days old they deposit their droppings over the edge of the nest. Young canaries leave the nest at about 18 days old, although they cannot usually feed themselves. If the hen starts nest building again, when the chicks are around 15 days old, it is best to put them – still in the nest pan – on the floor at the opposite end of the cage. A new nest pan can be fixed in the original position for the hen to lay her second clutch of eggs. When the chicks are moving freely about the floor of the cage you should watch to see if the cock or the hen objects to their behaviour. If so, refit the wire divider and put the chicks in the opposite end of the cage. The cock will feed them through the wire mesh.

Now in their own end of the cage, the chicks can learn to feed themselves. A feeding board – a small platform about 25mm (1 inch) above the cage floor – can help. Various foods placed on the board will tempt the chicks to try them. At this stage, no perches should be fitted to the side of the cage which houses the chicks.

When the chicks are capable of feeding themselves (around 21 days) they can be moved to another cage away from their parents. This move should not be made on the basis of how old the chicks are. You must know that they can feed themselves. The feeding board, which they will be used to, can be moved with them. When they are feeding well, a perch can be fitted in the cage – but

Coloured – Gold ground